Foreword: An American Artist

impler Times is not just another coloring book but a treasure and gift from one of today's most inspiring artists and craftsmen who brings his passion for art, history, family, and country to every single page.

I had the great privilege of working with Jim Shore many years ago during my time as an executive in the gift industry. Jim introduced me to a world of design and a creative process that continues to inspire me to this day. His design style and down-to-earth personality have inspired millions of people around the world for many years, but more importantly taught us all how to celebrate the rich design heritage found in the world of quilting and folk art. As an artist and designer, my appreciation for Jim's ability to celebrate the past while introducing a new, unique, and inspiring art style goes beyond words.

As a colorist, you will not only find endless hours of inspirational coloring in the pages of *Simpler Times* but also an opportunity to celebrate the patterns and motifs rich in quilting and folk-art history. These folk-art themes are all very much alive and celebrated today deep in the heart of Lancaster County, Pennsylvania—the home of Fox Chapel Publishing.

Simpler Times is a rare opportunity to follow the hands of a master artisan. As president of Fox Chapel Publishing, I'm grateful to Jim for sharing this amazing portfolio of his designs that can be admired and colored for years to come by all ages. My heartfelt thanks to Jim for sharing his deep passion for history and the people and art that have inspired him over the years.

Fox Chapel Publishing is headquartered in the heart of Amish country in Lancaster County, Pennsylvania. Our company and community have a deep appreciation for Jim's work and his passion for preserving the rich heritage and ethics of a land and people who continue to celebrate the importance of simpler times!

—David Miller
President, Fox Chapel Publishing
Mount Joy, Pennsylvania

You will find Amish quilts for sale throughout Pennsylvania Dutch country. This quilt auction benefitted a local fire company in Lancaster County, where Fox Chapel Publishing is headquartered.

Welcome to Old-Time Fun!

It's time to take a deep breath and enjoy coloring designs that bring back a simpler time. Each piece has folksy details that I hope you find joy in coloring.

The images in this coloring book are the result of a two-step process. First, there's the subject or character itself—a Santa or a landscape or birds—drawn in a folk-art style with slightly exaggerated proportions. Then comes the fun part! I've decorated them with design motifs drawn from folk-art traditions. These motifs come from quilting, rosemaling, fraktur, and what we today call Pennsylvania Dutch. It's a combination I find exciting, creating new designs with roots in our shared past.

I've been an artist all my life, and some of my earliest memories are drawing pictures for my mom. I can't explain it; it just comes naturally to me. My initial style was photorealism. I was mostly a painter, working in oils and acrylics. My early work as a young, starving artist included portraits and stamp designs. I even did a few covers for local phone books in that realistic style. But I was always drawn to folk art. I loved the idea of ordinary folks creating something beautiful out of things at hand—wood, tin, stone, or scraps of cloth. They didn't do it for money or fame; they were just driven to create. So I adopted folk art in my work. To be clear, I'm not a folk artist. My work combines multiple folk-art traditions. It's a style that resonates with me and I think with most folks. I enjoy taking the elements of our shared history and weaving them together to create something unique and new.

A COLORFUL LIFE

Coloring is something I've done all my life. I remember doing it with my brothers after school, sharing and competing while we laughed together. With 6 kids and 14 grandkids, I've had plenty of experience since, teaching and experimenting with crayons, pencils, watercolors, and the like. And now you could say it's my day job! It's a craft I'm passionate about, and I know I'm not alone. I believe people are driven to create and are drawn to color. It's just the nature of things, part of who we are, a part of being human.

There are hex signs on many barns in Pennsylvania Dutch country. Some folks believe they are symbols of happiness and good fortune.

Something you might see in your grandmother's attic—a painted chest showing the rosemaling technique.

My Work Space

I built my studio myself, so I like to think it's exactly what I need. It's a big, open area that measures about 35' x 50' (11 x 15m). It has tall, gabled ceilings. There's a floor-to-ceiling stone fireplace in the middle of the room that's sort of the centerpiece. And there are 20' (11m) windows on three sides with a kitchen on the fourth side. I have plenty of light and easy access to coffee.

Plentiful coffee helps because it can get pretty busy in here—you might say I like to have a lot going on! At any given moment I can have a dozen or so projects in the works. These run the gamut from bronze casting to stonecutting to glass molding, with characters ranging from Santa Claus to Abraham Lincoln to Tinker Bell. I love it! That variety and activity creates its own sort of energy, a combination of media and design that keeps my mind stimulated. Anyone else might walk in and think it's total chaos, but it's perfect for me, and I always know exactly where everything is . . . mostly.

I think that kind of active, multitasking work environment inspires and influences my art. My work combines elements from different folk-art traditions. I use quilting designs and quilt blocks as a foundation, of course, but I also draw on images from rosemaling, fraktur, and designs based on what we now call Pennsylvania Dutch. I find that mixture of different elements exciting. Creating different combinations keeps the eye moving over the entire work. That movement is what I think makes everything interesting. Creating a visual energy and levels of discovery ensures that there's always something new to see every time you look. That's really what I strive for in every finished design. I have a rule of thumb when I look at one of my pieces. If my eye comes to rest on any one element, no matter how wonderful or exciting that element is, it's wrong and out of place and needs to be changed.

The space where my hardest-working hours and most inspiring artistic moments are spent.

A view of the figurines I've enjoyed creating.

Tools for Coloring

I use a wide range of **colored pencils**. There are, of course, many brands and colors available. I like to use Prismacolor pencils, which can be purchased at your local craft store or online.

Colored pencils can produce a variety of effects, everything from a very saturated color to subtle color. Changing the pressure and repetition of strokes will get the density you want to achieve.

While a color wheel can be useful, it's more fun to choose the colors that inspire you and give you joy.

You may want to try using other tools to color the images in this book. The **markers** most commonly used for coloring are either alcohol-based or water-based. (Oil-based markers are typically used for surfaces other than paper.) One advantage to using alcohol-based markers is that they will not warp or buckle thinner paper the way water-based markers will.

Gel pens are perfect for enhancing and embellishing colored pieces. Because they are pens with fine-tip points, it would be very time-consuming to color an entire page with them; however, gel pens can be used to accentuate smaller areas in many different and fun ways. Try using them to add little pops of vibrant colors to a piece you've completed with markers or colored pencils.

TIP!

Markers sometimes bleed through coloring pages. Put a scrap page underneath your design to catch any marker or paint bleed-through and prevent it from getting onto other coloring pages or your table.

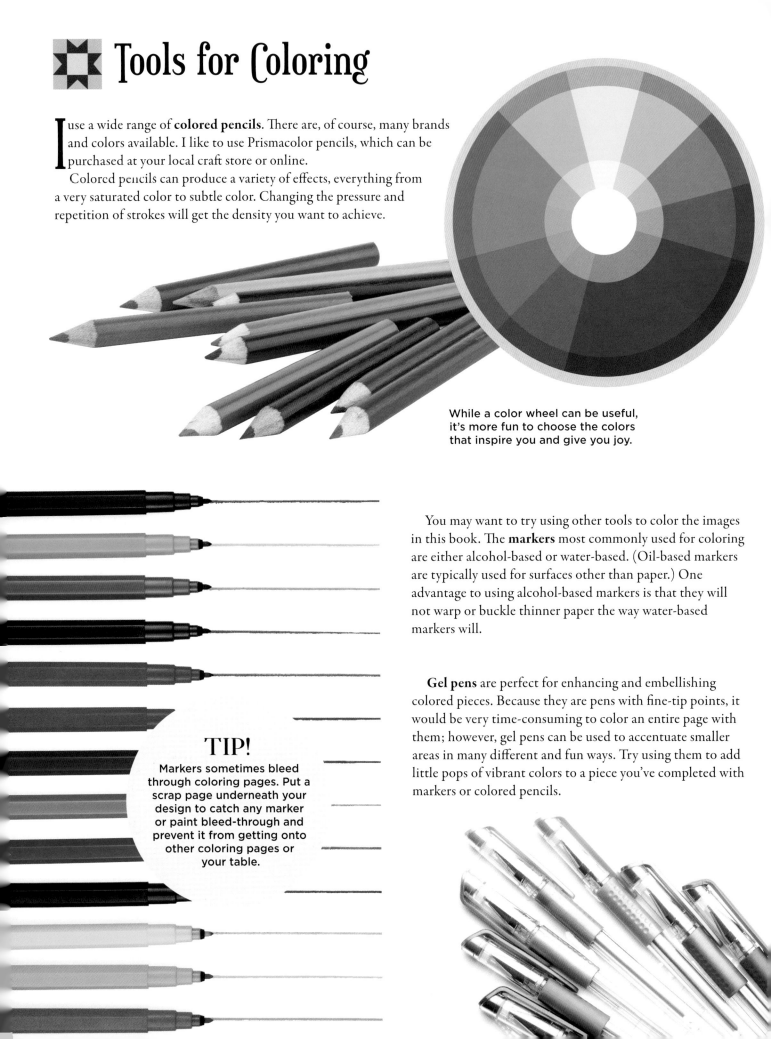

Other Handy Tools

One of my favorite tools is a **stump**. A stump is a hard paper stick that is pointed and shaped similar to a pencil. It's used in blending color in charcoal, pastel, or colored pencil. A stump can be used to manipulate and soften colors once they're applied to the paper.

Other tools I use include the **eraser stick** or battery-operated eraser, and an **eraser shield**. A nice eraser lets you remove any trace of a misplaced line or remove some color to create lighter shades.

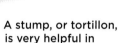

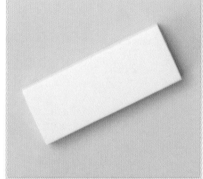

A stump, or tortillon, is very helpful in blending colors.

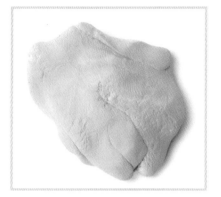

Kneaded eraser

Hard white eraser

If you've made a mistake with your colored pencil, you have lots of options. A **kneaded eraser** can be formed into any shape to help fit into small areas. Another option is a smooth, hard **white eraser**, which is useful for tough-to-erase colored pencils, and it won't leave behind colored eraser smudges on your paper. You can also get erasers in easy-to-use "mechanical pencil" form (also called eraser sticks) that are in a tube, and you can click out more eraser as you need it. They even make **eraser pencils**! A **sand eraser**, such as this one at left, is perfect for correcting mistakes in colored pencil or even ink. It can also bring back highlights, assist in blending, and bring back the texture of the paper when multiple layers of colored pencil have been applied.

Eraser pencil

Sand eraser

Another great tool is an **eraser shield**. It's used to erase small, precise areas without erasing more than you want. Only what's in the opening gets erased, and the shield protects the areas around it from being erased.

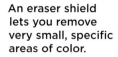

An eraser shield lets you remove very small, specific areas of color.

Techniques

I use several techniques when coloring: shading, highlighting, and blending. Each one helps bring an image to life.

Shading

When shading, you need to decide what tools and method you want to use. There are four general methods. The first method creates the most realistic effect.

METHOD 1: Pick two similar shades from the same color family and use them together: a base color (lighter color) and a shade color (darker color).

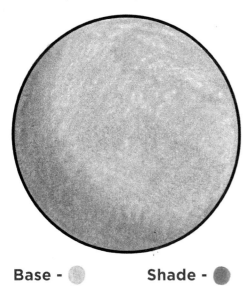

Base - ●   **Shade -** ●

METHOD 2: Use varying degrees of pressure with a single coloring tool to make the shaded part darker than the rest.

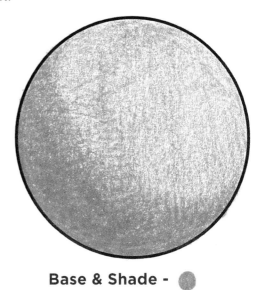

Base & Shade - ●

METHOD 3: Add black or gray where you want shading, or a totally different color than the one you're using as a base.

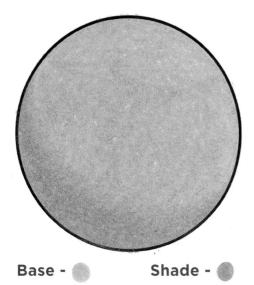

Base - ●   **Shade -** ●

METHOD 4: Use line techniques like stippling or crosshatching with ink or marker over colored pencil.

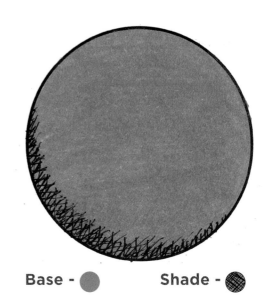

Base - ●   **Shade -** ●

Highlighting

A simple way to add highlights to your coloring is to use a white gel pen (for strong highlights) or white colored pencil (for subtle highlights). You could also use a kneaded eraser to pick up some of the base color where you would like to place a highlight; this works best with colored pencils. With a little planning, you can simply leave an area uncolored from the beginning to create a highlight.

Gel pen highlight

Colored pencil highlight

Highlight created by erasing

Blending

Blending allows you to seamlessly combine colors together to create visually stunning art. When blending, you can use any colors or media you want. Try starting with a monochromatic color scheme in one specific medium until you get comfortable with the process. Colored pencils are good tools for beginners to learn blending.

TIP
With colored pencils, tool sharpness and hand pressure make all the difference.

1 Start by laying down the light base color over the entire area you want to blend.

2 Use the dark shade to color lightly from the middle of the base color toward one edge of the shape. As you move father away from the area of your base shade, begin adding more pressure to your pencil, coloring the area more heavily.

3 Go back with the light base color and color over the base and dark shade areas. Repeat until you've created a nice, even coat of color.

See design on page 37.

See design on page 27.

See design on page 47.

See design on page 33.

See design on page 53.

See design on page 43.

11

See design on page 75.

See design on page 41.

See design on page 21.

See design on page 39.

See design on page 45.

See design on page 73.

15

See design on page 67.

Love Springs Eternal

See design on page 25.

Awaken the Day

With the new day comes
new strength and new thoughts.

–ELEANOR ROOSEVELT

AWAKEN THE DAY

My mother loved roosters. When I was a kid, I used to draw them for her for
birthdays, Mother's Day, and Christmas. So I have a lot of experience with
this subject, dating back to my crayon-on-butcher-paper period!

Concentrate all your thoughts upon the work at hand. The sun's rays do not burn until brought to a focus.

—Alexander Graham Bell

SUNBURST

There's nothing like a sunny day to raise your spirits. But if the weather doesn't cooperate, sometimes you have to create your own sunshine.

I'm dreaming of a white Christmas,
just like the ones I used to know.

—IRVING BERLIN

SNOWING BACK HOME

I grew up in a small town, a place where everyone knew everyone else and most folks
got along. When it snowed, it was like Christmas! We all got out in it and played.

I simply can't resist a cat, particularly a purring one. They are the cleanest, cunningest, and most intelligent things I know.

—MARK TWAIN

THREE WISE CATS

I have cats at my studio—they pretty much run the place to suit themselves. I'm just grateful they share the place with me!

There is no remedy
for love but to love more.

—HENRY DAVID THOREAU

LOVE SPRINGS ETERNAL

Sometimes my sense of humor can get me in trouble, like the time I gave my
wife, Jan, a kitchen sink for Valentine's Day. I've learned through experience to
keep things simple. A nice, heartfelt sentiment always does the trick.

The LORD gives strength to his people;
the LORD blesses his people with peace.

—Psalm 29:11

LIVE IN HARMONY

I've always loved this image of peace and promise. It's something I've used in different
ways many times in my art over the years. It always seems to turn out just right.

Wynkin, Blynkin, and Nod
one night sailed off in a wooden shoe;
Sailed off on a river of crystal light into a sea of dew.

—Eugene Field

WYNKIN, BLYNKIN, AND NOD

This nursery rhyme was a favorite with my kids. It's about adventure and travel
and faraway places. And in the end, about a peaceful night's sleep.

May your pockets be heavy and your heart be light. May good luck pursue you each morning and night.

—IRISH BLESSING

GOOD LUCK TO YOU (*ADH MÓR ORT*)
I've been to Ireland many times over the years. It's one of those places that doesn't disappoint, as beautiful and interesting in person as you always imagined it would be.

32

When you have eaten and are satisfied,
praise the LORD your God for the
good land he has given you.

—DEUTERONOMY 8:10

HOME IN THE VINEYARD

One of the great things about a vineyard scene is that it's beautiful no matter the season. Spring,
fall, or even winter, there's always some striking color or wonderful shape that captures the eye.

On the first day of
Christmas my true love gave to me
A partridge in a pear tree.

—FREDERIC AUSTIN

TWELVE DAYS SANTA

Over the years I've designed thousands of Santas, but this is one of my favorites. As kids, my brothers and I would sing this carol as a race, each trying to get to the "partridge in a pear tree" first. I never won!

Darkness cannot drive out darkness;
only light can do that. Hate cannot drive
out hate; only love can do that.

—Martin Luther King, Jr.

GUIDING LIGHT

Lighthouses have always fascinated me. Functional for sure—and necessary! But as
a powerful symbol of hope and guidance, they're even more meaningful.

What can you do to promote world peace?
Go home and love your family.

—MOTHER TERESA

DISTLEFINKS

Distlefinks are magical images in the hex signs of the Pennsylvania Dutch,
symbols of happiness and good fortune. And they're pretty, too!

Trains are wonderful. . . . To travel by train
is to see nature and human beings, towns and
churches and rivers, in fact, to see life.

—AGATHA CHRISTIE

THE PLACES YOU'LL GO

There's nothing quite like the sound of a train whistle in the distance. It makes you want
to pack your bags and head out to see the world! There are speedier ways to do that these
days, with cars and jets. But there's something still romantic about that sound.

Where flowers bloom, so does hope.

–LADY BIRD JOHNSON

BRIGHT AND BEAUTIFUL

I like to surround myself with color. Small accents remind me that the
world is a beautiful place and that spring is always on the way.

The great gift of Easter is hope.

—BASIL HUME

EASTER EGG ROLL

We have a big Easter egg hunt for the grandkids every year at my studio. It's
a family tradition that we treasure, and I know the kids love it. The best
part is that I hide the eggs—I get to be the Easter bunny!

Cats are a mysterious kind of folk.

—SIR WALTER SCOTT

FELICITY

I became a cat person late in life when my wife, Jan, found a wounded stray
that we nursed back to health. He quickly became a member of the family, and
I've been hooked ever since. I can't imagine life without them now!

Nobody has ever measured, not even poets,
how much the heart can hold.

–ZELDA FITZGERALD

HUGS AND KISSES

Artists have a reputation for being romantic. I'm not sure that's true, but I do have my moments.
They're not about big presents or grand gestures, just the simple things. Hugs and kisses.

I'm so glad I live in a world
where there are Octobers.

–L. M. MONTGOMERY

HARVEST BOUNTY

Fall is a time for color. And Mother Nature isn't timid with it! She uses orange with
purples and reds, and mixes in yellows with greens, and every now and then throws in a
surprise like fuchsia. I love those unexpected combinations, and I use them in my art.

"Look at the birds of the air; they do not sow or reap or store away in barns, and yet your heavenly Father feeds them. Are you not much more valuable than they? Can any one of you by worrying add a single hour to your life?"

—MATTHEW 6:26-27

FLYING FREE

I've always been fascinated by birds. They're colorful symbols of flight and freedom. I've been known to sit on my porch and watch them for hours.

Santa Claus is anyone who loves
another and seeks to make them happy;
who gives himself by thought or word
or deed in every gift that he bestows.

—EDWIN OSGOOD GROVER

SHARE THE SPIRIT

I like to have a lot going on in my art. The trick is to create a balance between a lot of different colors
and elements, and a flow that keeps the eye moving over the entire piece, taking it all in at once.

A true conservationist is a man who knows
that the world is not given by his fathers,
but borrowed from his children.

–JOHN JAMES AUDUBON

LADY OF THE LAKE

Nature uses color in unexpected ways sometimes. Mostly it creates an
almost perfect balance, where different shades and hues blend together in
harmony. But every now and then something really stands out!

Sail away from the safe harbor.
Catch the trade winds in your sails.
Explore! Dream! Discover!

—MARK TWAIN

THE WIND AT MY BACK

I guess with a family name like Shore, I was destined to love the sea. Over the years,
it's been a great source of inspiration—the color, the scale, and the subtle complexity.
It captures my imagination, and it's been a favorite theme in my work.

Double, double toil and trouble;
fire burn and caldron bubble.

–WILLIAM SHAKESPEARE

WICKEDNESS AWAITS

I love Halloween! Over the years, it's been the inspiration for some of the best and most
unique folk art. The images and themes can be ghoulish and gruesome, of course, but
there's an underlying sense of humor and fun that makes all the gloom go away.

Never give up listening to the sounds of birds.

–JOHN JAMES AUDUBON

BEAUTY IN THE AIR

Cardinals can be meaningful symbols, nature's messengers of comfort or connection
or hope. My father took me aside once to point out a cardinal perched in the snow. We
looked together in silence, a beautiful scene that connects us even now.

Thanksgiving is the holiday
that encompasses all others.
All of them . . . are in one way or
another about being thankful.

—JONATHAN SAFRAN FOER

GRATITUDE

Thanksgiving is rich in great imagery, everything from Pilgrims to the *Mayflower* or a cornucopia
or two, but it's not just the imagery I love. It's the color. It's the time of year when nature
combines reds, purples, oranges, and the like in ways a poor artist can only dream of! There's
nothing like the rich natural palette of fall, inspiring and humbling at the same time.

You haven't seen a tree until
you've seen its shadow from the sky.

—AMELIA EARHART

LIGHTER THAN AIR

I've never been up in a hot-air balloon. It's one of my ambitions, though, to sail over the
countryside in silence, powered only by the wind. If only I weren't terrified of heights!

"Have you come to sing pumpkin carols?"

–IT'S THE GREAT PUMPKIN, CHARLIE BROWN

MISCHIEF IN THE MAKING

I love how everything flows in this cat and pumpkin design: the stark geometrics
of the quilt patterning against the floral rosemaling motifs in the background and
border. There's an energy there that keeps the eye moving across the entire piece.

What is the charm that makes
old things so sweet?

—SARAH DOUDNEY

CARRIAGE RIDE

Folk art can look deceptively simple. It's often considered somewhat plain and
straightforward, but the combination of elements, color, and composition can create
levels of discovery so that you see something new every time you look.

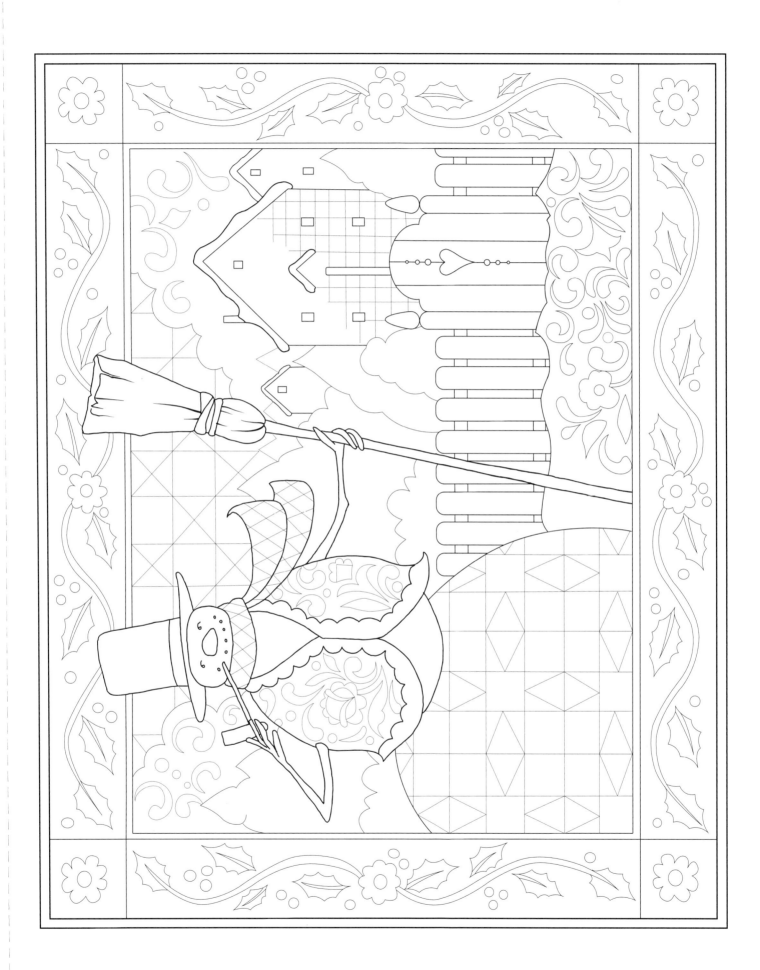

In seed time learn,
in harvest teach, in winter enjoy.

–WILLIAM BLAKE

WONDERLAND

When I first had the idea for a collection of snowman designs, some people said I couldn't
make them very interesting. After all, a snowman is really just three white balls! But with
a little imagination and some artistic license, I think I've made it work pretty well!

May the blessing of Light be on you,
light without and light within.

—IRISH BLESSING

LIGHT OF FAITH

No matter how far away we live from a coastline, images of the sea seem to speak to us. As Americans, our ancestors all came across the sea one way or another. Our earliest history is deeply connected to it, and so images of lighthouses and sailing ships are important links to our past.

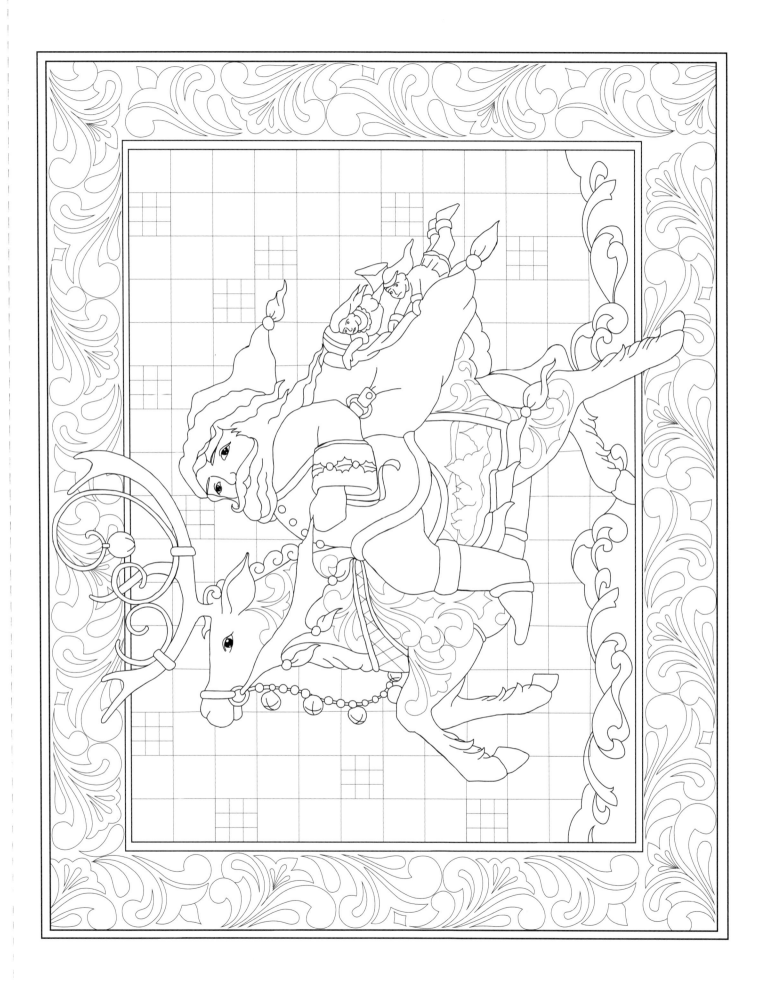

When we recall Christmas past,
we usually find that the simplest things—
not the great occasions—give off the
greatest glow of happiness.

—BOB HOPE

NEXT STOP, THE ROOFTOP

I love the composition of this design, the sense of movement—you can almost feel the wind
in your face. And the toys in Santa's bag hanging on for dear life adds to the adventure!

The country life is to be preferred,
for there we see the works of God.

—WILLIAM PENN

A GRAND TRADITION

My art is really a two-step process. The first step is choosing the subject itself—Santa or an angel or a
farm animal—and creating the basic shape, usually with a subtly out-of-proportion, folk-art feel. Then
comes the fun part! Using motifs taken from various folk-art traditions like quilting and Pennsylvania
Dutch, I decorate and enhance the subject. It's a style I love, and I can't imagine ever tiring of it.